Graphic Pattern AFGHANS

All-over patterns of geometric shapes create seven eye-catching afghans with fresh appeal. Each is easy to crochet using medium weight yarn.

LEISURE ARTS, INC. • Maumelle, Arkansas

ZIPPERS

EASY

Finished Size: 57" x 69¾" (145 cm x 177 cm)

Shopping List

Yarn (Medium Weight) MEDIUM 4

(7 ounces, 364 yards
(198 grams, 333 meters)
per skein):

- ☐ Green - 5 skeins
- ☐ Dk Green - 3 skeins

Crochet Hook

- ☐ Size G (4 mm)
  or size needed for gauge

Gauge Information

In pattern,
2 repeats (20 sts) = 6" (15.25 cm);
Rows 1-12 = 6¼" (16 cm)

Gauge Swatch: 6" wide x 6¼" high
(15.25 x 16 cm)

With Dk Green, ch 21.

Rows 1-12: Work same as Body, page 4;
at end of Row 12, do **not** change colors:
20 sc.

Finish off.

Stitch Guide

TREBLE CROCHET ***(abbreviated tr)***

YO twice, insert hook in st indicated, YO and pull up a loop (4 loops on hook), (YO and draw through 2 loops on hook) 3 times.

DOUBLE TREBLE CROCHET ***(abbreviated dtr)***

YO 3 times, insert hook in st indicated, YO and pull up a loop (5 loops on hook), (YO and draw through 2 loops on hook) 4 times.

SINGLE CROCHET 2 TOGETHER ***(abbreviated sc2tog)***

Pull up a loop in next ch and in next FPdc, YO and draw through all 3 loops on hook **(counts as one sc)**.

FRONT POST DOUBLE CROCHET ***(abbreviated FPdc)***

YO, insert hook from **front** to **back** around post of st indicated ***(Fig. A)***, YO and pull up a loop (3 loops on hook), (YO and draw through 2 loops on hook) twice.

BACK POST DOUBLE CROCHET ***(abbreviated BPdc)***

YO, insert hook from **back** to **front** around post of st indicated ***(Fig. A)***, YO and pull up a loop (3 loops on hook), (YO and draw through 2 loops on hook) twice.

Fig. A

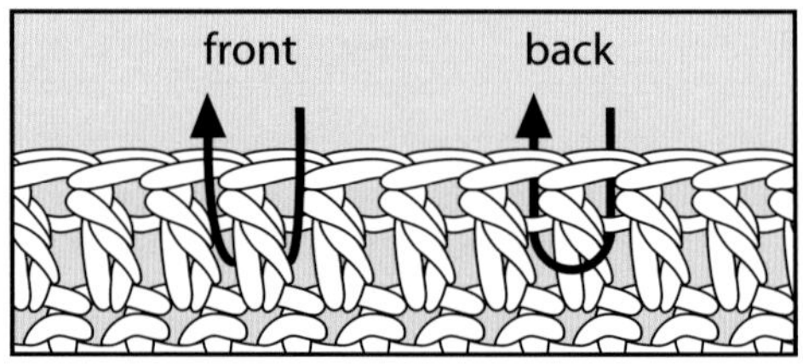

Body

With Dk Green, ch 181.

Row 1 (Right side)**:** Sc in second ch from hook and in next ch, hdc in next 2 chs, dc in next 2 chs, tr in next 2 chs, ★ dtr in next ch, **(**ch 5, slip st in next st **(counts as one dtr, now and throughout))**, sc in next 2 chs, hdc in next 2 chs, dc in next 2 chs, tr in next 2 chs; repeat from ★ across to last 2 chs, dtr in last 2 chs changing to Green in last dtr ***(Fig. 3, page 30)***: 180 sts.

Note: Loop a short piece of yarn around any stitch to mark Row 1 as **right** side.

Row 2: Ch 1, turn; sc in first 2 dtr, hdc in next 2 tr, dc in next 2 dc, tr in next 2 hdc, dtr in next 2 sc, ★ sc in next 2 dtr, hdc in next 2 tr, dc in next 2 dc, tr in next 2 hdc, dtr in next 2 sc; repeat from ★ across.

Row 3: Ch 1, turn; sc in first 2 dtr, hdc in next 2 tr, dc in next 2 dc, tr in next 2 hdc, ★ dtr in next sc, ch 5, slip st in next sc, sc in next 2 dtr, hdc in next 2 tr, dc in next 2 dc, tr in next 2 hdc; repeat from ★ across to last 2 sc, dtr in last 2 sc changing to Dk Green in last dtr.

Rows 4 and 5: Repeat Rows 2 and 3, changing to Green at end of Row 5.

Rows 6 and 7: Repeat Rows 2 and 3.

Row 8: Ch 1, turn; sc in first 2 dtr, hdc in next 2 tr, dc in next 2 dc, tr in next 2 hdc, dtr in next 2 sc, ★ sc in next 2 dtr, hdc in next 2 tr, dc in next 2 dc, tr in next 2 hdc, dtr in next 2 sc; repeat from ★ across, changing to Green in last dtr.

Row 9: Ch 1, turn; 2 sc in first dtr, sc in next st and in each st across: 181 sc.

Row 10: Ch 4 **(counts as first dc plus ch 1, now and throughout)**, turn; skip next sc, dc in next sc, ★ ch 1, skip next sc, dc in next sc; repeat from ★ across: 91 dc and 90 chs.

Row 11: Ch 4, turn; (work FPdc around next dc, ch 1) across to last dc, dc in last dc.

Row 12: Ch 1, turn; sc in first dc, sc2tog, sc in each ch and in each FPdc across changing to Dk Green in last sc: 180 sc.

Row 13: Ch 1, turn; sc in first 2 sc, hdc in next 2 sc, dc in next 2 sc, tr in next 2 sc, ★ dtr in next sc, ch 5, slip st in next sc, sc in next 2 sc, hdc in next 2 sc, dc in next 2 sc, tr in next 2 sc; repeat from ★ across to last 2 sc, dtr in last 2 sc changing to Green in last dtr made.

Rows 14-128: Repeat Rows 2-13, 9 times; then repeat Rows 2-8 once **more**.

Border

Rnd 1: Ch 1, turn; 2 sc in first dtr, skip next st, sc in each st across to last sc, 3 sc in last sc; work 221 sc evenly spaced across ends of rows to beginning ch; working in free loops of beginning ch ***(Fig. 1, page 30)***, 3 sc in first ch, skip next ch, sc in each ch across to ch at base of first sc, 3 sc in ch at base of first sc; work 221 sc evenly spaced across ends of rows; sc in same st as first sc; join with slip st to first sc: 808 sc.

Rnd 2: Ch 4, dc in same st as joining, ch 1, ★ skip next sc, (dc in next sc, ch 1, skip next sc) across to center sc of next corner 3-sc group, (dc, ch 1) 3 times in center sc; repeat from ★ 2 times **more**, skip next sc, (dc in next sc, ch 1, skip next sc) across, dc in same st as first dc, ch 1; join with slip st to first dc: 415 dc and 415 ch-1 sps.

Rnd 3: Ch 4, **turn**; (work BPdc around next dc, ch 1) around, working (BPdc, ch 1) twice around center dc of each corner 3-dc group; join with slip st to first dc: 419 sts and 419 ch-1 sps.

Rnd 4: Ch 1, turn; sc in each st and in each ch-1 sp around working 3 sc in each corner ch-1 sp; join with slip st to first sc, finish off.

Rnd 5: With **right** side facing, join Dk Green with slip st in any sc; ch 1, working from **left** to **right**, work reverse sc in each sc around ***(Figs. 4a-d, page 30)***; join with slip st to first st, finish off.

LIGHTNING BOLTS

EASY

Finished Size: 44" x 61" (112 cm x 155 cm)

Shopping List

Yarn (Medium Weight) MEDIUM 4

(4 ounces, 203 yards

(113 grams, 186 meters)

per skein**)**:

- ☐ Cream - 7 skeins
- ☐ Green - 7 skeins

Crochet Hook

- ☐ Size G (4 mm)

  or size needed for gauge

Gauge Information

In pattern,

2 repeats (20 sts) and

Rows 1-13 = 4¾" (12 cm)

Gauge Swatch: 4¾" (12 cm) square

With Green, ch 21.

Rows 1-13: Work same as Body, page 8; at end of Row 13, do **not** change colors: 20 sc.

Finish off.

Stitch Guide

TREBLE CROCHET ***(abbreviated tr)***
YO twice, insert hook in st indicated, YO and pull up a loop (4 loops on hook), (YO and draw through 2 loops on hook) 3 times.

DOUBLE TREBLE CROCHET ***(abbreviated dtr)***
YO 3 times, insert hook in st indicated, YO and pull up a loop (5 loops on hook), (YO and draw through 2 loops on hook) 4 times.

Each row is worked across the length of the Afghan.

Body

With Green, ch 242.

Row 1 (Right side)**:** Sc in second ch from hook and in each ch across: 241 sc.

Note: Loop a short piece of yarn around any stitch to mark Row 1 as **right** side.

Row 2: Ch 4 **(counts as first dc plus ch 1, now and throughout)**, turn; skip next sc, dc in next sc, ★ ch 1, skip next sc, dc in next sc; repeat from ★ across: 121 dc and 120 ch-1 sps.

Row 3: Ch 1, turn; sc in first dc and in each ch-1 sp and each dc across changing to Cream in last sc ***(Fig. 3, page 30)***: 241 sc.

Row 4: Ch 5 **(counts as first dtr, now and throughout)**, turn; dtr in next sc, tr in next 2 sc, dc in next 2 sc, hdc in next 2 sc, sc in next 2 sc, ★ **(**slip st in next sc, ch 5 **(counts as one dtr))**, dtr in next sc, tr in next 2 sc, dc in next 2 sc, hdc in next 2 sc, sc in next 2 sc; repeat from ★ across to last sc, slip st in last sc.

Row 5: Ch 4, with Green ch 1 **(first dtr made)**, turn; ★ dtr in next 2 sc, tr in next 2 hdc, dc in next 2 dc, hdc in next 2 tr, sc in next 2 dtr; repeat from ★ across changing to Cream in last sc.

Row 6: Ch 1, turn; sc in first st and in each st across.

Row 7: Ch 4, turn; skip next sc, dc in next sc, ★ ch 1, skip next sc, dc in next sc; repeat from ★ across: 121 dc and 120 ch-1 sps.

Row 8: Ch 1, turn; sc in first dc and in each ch-1 sp and each dc across changing to Green in last sc: 241 sc.

Row 9: Ch 1, turn; sc in first 2 sc, hdc in next 2 sc, dc in next 2 sc, tr in next 2 sc, dtr in next sc, **(**ch 5, slip st in next sc **(counts as one dtr))**, ★ sc in next 2 sc, hdc in next 2 sc, dc in next 2 sc, tr in next 2 sc, dtr in next sc, ch 5, slip st in next sc; repeat from ★ across to last sc, sc in last sc changing to Cream.

Row 10: Ch 5, turn; ★ sc in next 2 dtr, hdc in next 2 tr, dc in next 2 dc, tr in next 2 hdc, dtr in next 2 sc; repeat from ★ across changing to Green in last dtr.

Row 11: Ch 1, turn; sc in first st and in each st across.

Row 12: Ch 4, turn; skip next sc, dc in next sc, ★ ch 1, skip next sc, dc in next sc; repeat from ★ across: 121 dc and 120 ch-1 sps.

Row 13: Ch 1, turn; sc in first dc and in each ch-1 sp and each dc across changing to Cream in last sc: 241 sc.

Rows 14-113: Repeat Rows 4-13, 10 times; at end of Row 113, do **not** change colors; finish off Green.

Border

Rnd 1: With **right** side facing, join Cream with slip st in first sc; ch 3 **(counts as first dc, now and throughout)**, 2 dc in same st, dc in next sc and in each sc across to last sc, 5 dc in last sc; work 195 dc evenly spaced across ends of rows to beginning ch; working in free loops of beginning ch ***(Fig. 1, page 30)***, 5 dc in first ch, dc in each ch across to ch at base of first sc, 5 dc in ch at base of first sc; work 195 dc evenly spaced across ends of rows; 2 dc in same st as first dc; join with slip st to first dc: 888 dc.

Rnd 2: Ch 3, 2 dc in same st as joining, dc in next dc and in each dc across to center dc of next corner 5-dc group, ★ 5 dc in center dc, dc in next dc and in each dc across to center dc of next corner 5-dc group; repeat from ★ 2 times **more**, 2 dc in same st as first dc; join with slip st to first dc: 904 dc.

Rnd 3: Ch 4, (dc, ch 1) 3 times in same st as joining, skip next dc, ★ (dc in next dc, ch 1, skip next dc) across to center dc of next corner 5-dc group, (dc, ch 1) 4 times in center dc, skip next dc; repeat from ★ 2 times **more**, (dc in next dc, ch 1, skip next dc) across; join with slip st to first dc: 464 dc and 464 chs.

Rnd 4: Ch 1, sc in same st as joining and in next ch, sc in next dc, 3 sc in next corner ch, ★ sc in next dc and in each ch across to next corner ch, 3 sc in corner ch; repeat from ★ 2 times **more**, sc in each dc and in each ch across; join with slip st to first sc, finish off: 936 sc.

Rnd 5: With **right** side facing, join Green with slip st in any sc; working from **left** to **right**, work reverse sc in each sc around ***(Figs. 4a-d, page 30)***; join with slip st to first st, finish off.

SKYLINE

EASY

Finished Size: 60" x 74" (152.5 cm x 188 cm)

Shopping List

Yarn (Medium Weight) MEDIUM 4

(3.5 ounces, 208 yards
(100 grams, 190 meters)
per skein):

- ☐ Grey - 9 skeins
- ☐ Navy - 8 skeins

Crochet Hook

- ☐ Size I (5.5 mm)
  or size needed for gauge

Gauge Information

In pattern,
12 sts and Rows 1-10 = 4" (10 cm);

Gauge Swatch: 4" (10 cm) square
With Grey, ch 16.
Rows 1-10: Work same as Body, page 12: 14 sc.
Finish off.

Stitch Guide

TREBLE CROCHET ***(abbreviated tr)***

YO twice, insert hook in st indicated, YO and pull up a loop (4 loops on hook), (YO and draw through 2 loops on hook) 3 times.

DOUBLE TREBLE CROCHET ***(abbreviated dtr)***

YO 3 times, insert hook in st indicated, YO and pull up a loop (5 loops on hook), (YO and draw through 2 loops on hook) 4 times.

FRONT POST DOUBLE CROCHET ***(abbreviated FPdc)***

YO, working in **front** of next sc, insert hook from **front** to **back** around post of st indicated ***(Fig. A, page 4)***, YO and pull up a loop (3 loops on hook), (YO and draw through 2 loops on hook) twice. Skip sc behind FPdc.

Body

With Grey, ch 168, place marker in third ch from hook for st placement.

Row 1 (Right side)**:** Dc in fourth ch from hook **(3 skipped chs count as first dc)** and in each ch across, changing to Navy in last dc ***(Fig. 3, page 30)***: 166 dc.

Note: Loop a short piece of yarn around any stitch to mark Row 1 as **right** side.

Row 2: Ch 1, turn; sc in each dc across.

Row 3: Ch 3 **(counts as first dc, now and throughout)**, turn; ★ dc in next 4 sc, ch 4, skip next 4 sc; repeat from ★ across to last 5 sc, dc in last 5 sc: 86 dc and 80 chs.

Row 4: Ch 1, turn; sc in each dc and in each ch across changing to Grey in last sc: 166 sc.

Row 5: Ch 3, turn; dc in next sc, work FPdc around each of next 2 dc one row **below**, ★ dc in next sc, working in **front** of previous 2 rows, dtr in 4 skipped sc on Row 2, dc in next sc on Row 4, work FPdc around each of next 2 dc one row **below**; repeat from ★ across to last 2 sc, dc in last 2 sc changing to Navy in last dc.

Row 6: Ch 1, turn; sc in each st across.

Row 7: Ch 7 **(counts as first dc plus ch 4)**, turn; skip next 4 sc, ★ dc in next 4 sc, ch 4, skip next 4 sc; repeat from ★ across to last sc, dc in last sc: 82 dc and 84 chs.

Row 8: Ch 1, turn; sc in each dc and in each ch across changing to Grey in last sc: 166 sc.

Row 9: Ch 3, turn; working in **front** of previous 2 rows, dtr in 4 skipped sc on Row 6, ★ dc in next sc, work FPdc around each of next 2 dc one row **below**, dc in next sc, working in **front** of previous 2 rows, dtr in 4 skipped sc on Row 6; repeat from ★ across to last sc, dc in last sc changing to Navy.

Rows 10-173: Repeat Rows 2-9, 20 times; then repeat Rows 2-5 once **more**; at end of Row 173, do **not** change colors.

Border

Rnd 1: Ch 1, do **not** turn; 2 sc in last dc made; work 212 sc evenly spaced across ends of rows; working in free loops of beginning ch ***(Fig. 1, page 30)***, 3 sc in first ch, sc in each ch across to marked ch, 3 sc in marked ch, remove marker; work 212 sc evenly spaced across ends of rows, 3 sc in first dc on Row 173, sc in each st across and in same st as first sc; join with slip st to first sc: 764 sc.

Rnd 2: Ch 4 **(counts as first tr)**, 2 tr in same st as joining, ★ tr in next sc and in each sc across to center sc of next corner 3-sc group, 5 tr in center sc; repeat from ★ 2 times **more**, tr in next sc and in each sc across, 2 tr in same st as first tr; join with slip st to first tr changing to Navy ***(Fig. A)***: 780 tr.

Fig. A

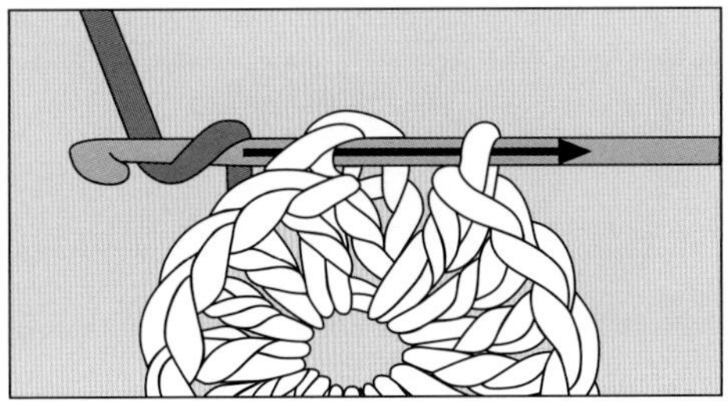

Rnd 3: Ch 3, 2 dc in same st as joining, ★ dc in next tr and in each tr across to center tr of next corner 5-tr group, 5 dc in center tr; repeat from ★ 2 times **more**, dc in next tr and in each tr around, 2 dc in same st as first dc; join with slip st to first dc changing to Grey: 796 dc.

Rnd 4: Ch 2 **(counts as first hdc)**, 2 hdc in same st as joining, ★ hdc in next dc and in each dc across to center dc of next corner 5-dc group, 5 hdc in center dc; repeat from ★ 2 times **more**, hdc in next dc and in each dc across, 2 hdc in same st as first hdc; join with slip st to first hdc changing to Navy: 812 hdc.

Rnd 5: Ch 1, sc in same st as joining, ch 1, (sc in next hdc, ch 1) around; join with slip st to first sc, finish off.

OCEAN WAVES

EASY

Finished Size: 46" x 57½" (117 cm x 146 cm)

Shopping List

Yarn (Medium Weight)

(6 ounces, 315 yards
(170.1 grams, 288 meters)
per skein**)**:

- ☐ White - 3 skeins
- ☐ Lt Blue - 2 skeins
- ☐ Dk Blue - 2 skeins
- ☐ Blue - 2 skeins

Crochet Hook

- ☐ Size G (4 mm)
  or size needed for gauge

Gauge Information

In pattern,
17 sts and Rows 1-14 = 5"
(12.75 cm) at highest point

Gauge Swatch: 8¼" x 5"
(21 cm x 12.75 cm)

With White, ch 29.

Rows 1-14: Work same as Body, page 16; at end of Row 14, do **not** change colors: 28 sts.

Finish off.

Stitch Guide

TREBLE CROCHET *(abbreviated tr)*
YO twice, insert hook in sc indicated, YO and pull up a loop (4 loops on hook), (YO and draw through 2 loops on hook) 3 times.

DOUBLE TREBLE CROCHET *(abbreviated dtr)*
YO 3 times, insert hook in st indicated, YO and pull up a loop (5 loops on hook), (YO and draw through 2 loops on hook) 4 times.

EXTRA LONG SINGLE CROCHET *(abbreviated ex LSC)*
Insert hook in st 2 rows **below** next st, YO and pull up a loop even with last st made, YO and draw through both loops on hook **(counts as one sc)**.

LONG SINGLE CROCHET *(abbreviated LSC)*
Insert hook in st on row **below** next st, YO and pull up a loop even with last st made, YO and draw through both loops on hook **(counts as one sc)**.

Body

With White, ch 141; place marker in second ch from hook for st placement.

Row 1: Sc in second ch from hook and in each ch across: 140 sc.

Row 2 (Right side)**:** Ch 1, turn; sc in first 2 sc, hdc in next sc, dc in next sc, tr in next sc, dtr in next 4 sc, tr in next sc, dc in next sc, hdc in next sc, ★ sc in next 4 sc, hdc in next sc, dc in next sc, tr in next sc, dtr in next 4 sc, tr in next sc, dc in next sc, hdc in next sc; repeat from ★ across to last 2 sc, sc in last 2 sc changing to Lt Blue in last sc ***(Fig. 3, page 30)***.

Note: Loop a short piece of yarn around any stitch to mark Row 2 as **right** side.

Row 3: Ch 1, turn; working in beginning ch, work ex LSC, work LSC, sc in next 10 sts, ★ work LSC, working in beginning ch, work ex LSC twice, work LSC, sc in next 10 sts; repeat from ★ across to last 2 sc, work LSC, work ex LSC.

Row 4: Ch 1, turn; sc in each st across.

Row 5: Ch 5 **(counts as first dtr)**, turn; dtr in next sc, tr in next sc, dc in next sc, hdc in next sc, sc in next 4 sc, hdc in next sc, dc in next sc, tr in next sc, ★ dtr in next 4 sc, tr in next sc, dc in next sc, hdc in next sc, sc in next 4 sc, hdc in next sc, dc in next sc, tr in next sc; repeat from ★ across to last 2 sc, dtr in last 2 sc changing to Blue in last dtr.

Row 6: Ch 1, turn; sc in first 5 sts, work LSC, work ex LSC twice, work LSC, ★ sc in next 10 sts, work LSC, work ex LSC twice, work LSC; repeat from ★ across to last 5 sts, sc in last 5 sts.

Row 7: Ch 1, turn; sc in each st across.

Row 8: Ch 1, turn; sc in first 2 sc, hdc in next sc, dc in next sc, tr in next sc, dtr in next 4 sc, tr in next sc, dc in next sc, hdc in next sc, ★ sc in next 4 sc, hdc in next sc, dc in next sc, tr in next sc, dtr in next 4 sc, tr in next sc, dc in next sc, hdc in next sc; repeat from ★ across to last 2 sc, sc in last 2 sc changing to Dk Blue in last sc.

Rows 9-11: Repeat Rows 3-5, changing to White at end of Row 11.

Rows 12-14: Repeat Rows 6-8, changing to Lt Blue at end of Row 14.

Rows 15-146: Repeat Rows 3-14, 11 times; at end of Row 146, do **not** change colors.

Row 147: Ch 1, turn; sc in each st across: do **not** finish off.

Border

Rnd 1: Ch 1, turn; 3 sc in first sc, sc in each sc across to last sc, 3 sc in last sc; sc evenly across ends of rows to beginning ch; working in free loops of beginning ch ***(Fig. 1, page 30)***, 3 sc in marked ch, remove marker, sc in each ch across to last ch, 3 sc in last ch; sc evenly across ends of rows; join with slip st to first sc.

Rnd 2: Ch 1, sc in each sc around working 3 sc in center sc of each corner 3-sc group; join with slip st to first sc.

Rnd 3: Ch 3 **(counts as first dc)**, dc in next sc and in each sc across to center sc of next corner 3-sc group, ★ 5 dc in center sc, dc in next sc and in each sc across to center sc of next corner 3-sc group; repeat from ★ 2 times **more**, dc in next sc and in each sc across; join with slip st to first dc.

Rnd 4: Ch 1, working in Back Loops Only ***(Fig. 2, page 30)***, sc in each dc around working 3 sc in center dc of each corner 5-dc group; join with slip st to **both** loops of first sc, finish off.

Rnd 5: With **right** side facing, join Dk Blue with slip st in any st; ch 1, working from **left** to **right**, work reverse sc in each sc around ***(Figs. 4a-d, page 30)***; join with slip st to first st, finish off.

RIPPLES

EASY

Finished Size: 43¾" x 62¼" (111 cm x 158 cm)

Shopping List

Yarn (Medium Weight) 4 MEDIUM

[5 ounces, 256 yards (141 grams, 234 meters) per skein**]**:

- ☐ Dk Grey - 5 skeins
- ☐ Black - 4 skeins

[4 ounces, 212 yards (113 grams, 194 meters) per skein**]**:

- ☐ Lt Grey - 5 skeins

Crochet Hook

- ☐ Size H (5 mm) **or** size needed for gauge

Gauge Information

In pattern, 16 sts = 4" (10 cm);
Rows 1-14 = 4½" (11.5 cm)
Each Strip = 4¾" (12 cm) wide

Gauge Swatch: 4" wide x 4½" high (10 cm x 11.5 cm)

Work same as Strip, page 20, through Row 14: 16 sc.

Stitch Guide

TREBLE CROCHET ***(abbreviated tr)***
YO twice, insert hook in sc indicated, YO and pull up a loop (4 loops on hook), (YO and draw through 2 loops on hook) 3 times.

Strip

(Make 5 Dk Grey and 4 Lt Grey)

Ch 17.

Row 1 (Right side)**:** Sc in second ch from hook and in next 2 chs, hdc in next 2 chs, dc in next 2 chs, tr in next 2 chs, dc in next 2 chs, hdc in next 2 chs, sc in last 3 chs: 16 sts.

Note: Loop a short piece of yarn around any stitch to mark Row 1 as **right** side **and** bottom edge.

Work in Back Loops Only on each row ***(Fig. 2, page 30)***.

Row 2: Ch 1, turn; sc in each st across.

Row 3: Ch 4 **(counts as first tr)**, turn; dc in next 2 sc, hdc in next 2 sc, sc in next 6 sc, hdc in next 2 sc, dc in next 2 sc, tr in last sc.

Row 4: Ch 1, turn; sc in each st across.

Row 5: Ch 1, turn; sc in first 3 sc, hdc in next 2 sc, dc in next 2 sc, tr in next 2 sc, dc in next 2 sc, hdc in next 2 sc, sc in last 3 sc.

Rows 6-189: Repeat Rows 2-5, 46 times.

Finish off.

Strip Edging

First Side

Row 1: With **right** side facing and working in ends of rows, join Black with sc in Row 1 ***(see Joining With Sc, page 30)***; work 240 sc evenly spaced across: 241 sc.

Row 2: Ch 1, turn; sc in each sc across; finish off.

Second Side

Joining in end of Row 189, repeat Strip Edging on opposite side.

Repeat for 6 inner Strips (3 Lt Grey and 3 Dk Grey).

For remaining Dk Grey Strips, work only First Side Edging on one Strip and only Second Side Edging on remaining Strip.

Assembly

Using diagram as a guide for placement, join Strips as follows:

With **wrong** sides and bottom edges of two Strips together, working through **inside** loops only of each sc on Strip Edgings, join Black with sc in first sc; sc in each sc across; finish off.

Join remaining Strips in same manner.

DIAGRAM

Border

Rnd 1: With **right** side facing and working across top edge, join Black with sc in first sc on Row 189; sc in same st and in each st across to Strip Edging; skip first row, sc in end of next row, sc in Strip Joining and in end of next row on next Strip Edging, skip last row, † sc in each st across to next Strip Edging, skip first row, sc in end of next row, sc in Strip Joining and in end of next row on next Strip Edging, skip last row †; repeat from † to † 6 times **more**, sc in each st across to last sc, 3 sc in last sc, sc in end of each row across outer Strip; working in free loops of beginning ch ***(Fig. 1, page 30)***, 3 sc in first ch, repeat from † to † 8 times, sc in each ch across to ch at base of first sc, 3 sc in ch at base of first sc; sc in end of each row across outer Strip; sc in same st as first sc; join with slip st to first sc.

Rnd 2: Ch 1, 3 sc in same st as joining, sc in each sc around working 3 sc in center sc of each corner 3-sc group; join with slip st to Back Loop Only of first sc.

Rnd 3: Ch 1, sc in Back Loop Only of each sc around working 3 sc in center sc of each corner 3-sc group; join with slip st through free loop of sc on Rnd 2 **and** in Front Loop Only of first sc ***(Fig. A)***.

Fig. A

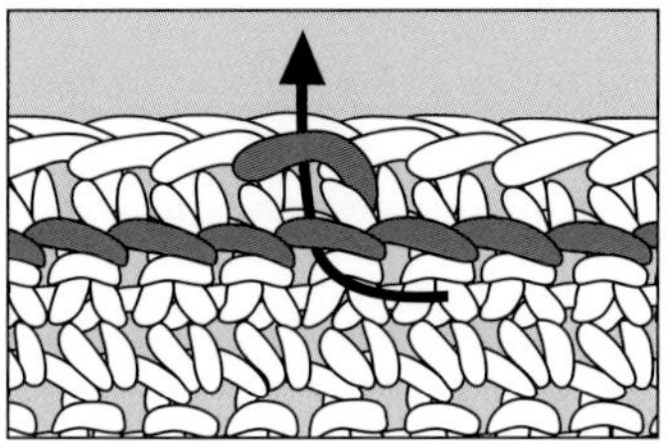

Rnd 4: Ch 1, working in free loops of sc on Rnd 2 **and** in Front Loops Only of sc on Rnd 3, sc in each sc around working 3 sc in center sc of each corner 3-sc group; join with slip st to **both** loops of first sc.

Rnd 5: Working in free loops of sc on Rnd 3, (slip st, ch 1, sc) in first sc, sc in each sc around working 3 sc in center sc of each corner 3-sc group; join with slip st to **both** loops of first sc, finish off.

SHADED VEES

EASY

Finished Size: 56" x 72" (142 cm x 183 cm)

Shopping List

Yarn (Medium Weight) MEDIUM 4

(5 ounces, 251 yards
(142 grams, 230 meters)
per skein**)**:

- ☐ Cream - 7 skeins
- ☐ Tan - 4 skeins
- ☐ Brown - 4 skeins

Crochet Hook

- ☐ Size H (5 mm)
  or size needed for gauge

Gauge Information

In pattern,
14 sts and Rows 1-12 = 4" (10 cm)

Gauge Swatch: 4" (10 cm) square

With Tan, ch 15.

Row 1: Hdc in third ch from hook **(2 skipped chs count as first hdc)** and in each ch across: 14 hdc.

Row 2: Ch 1, turn; sc in each hdc across.

Row 3: Ch 2 **(counts as first hdc)**, turn; hdc in next st and in each st across.

Rows 4 and 5: Ch 1, turn; sc in each st across.

Row 6: Ch 3 **(counts as first dc)**, turn; dc in next sc and in each sc across.

Row 7: Repeat Row 3.

Rows 8-12: Repeat Rows 2-6.

Finish off.

Stitch Guide

TREBLE CROCHET ***(abbreviated tr)***

YO twice, insert hook in st indicated, YO and pull up a loop (4 loops on hook), (YO and draw through 2 loops on hook) 3 times.

DOUBLE TREBLE CROCHET ***(abbreviated dtr)***

YO 3 times, insert hook in st indicated, YO and pull up a loop (5 loops on hook), (YO and draw through 2 loops on hook) 4 times.

LONG SINGLE CROCHET ***(abbreviated LSC)***

Working **around** previous row or rnd, insert hook in st one row or rnd **below** next st, YO and pull up a loop even with last sc made, YO and draw through both loops on hook.

Body

With Brown, ch 182; place marker in second ch from hook for st placement.

Row 1 (Right side)**:** Hdc in third ch from hook **(2 skipped chs count as first hdc)** and in next ch, ch 1, ★ skip next ch, hdc in next 5 chs, ch 1; repeat from ★ across to last 4 chs, skip next ch, hdc in last 3 chs: 151 hdc and 30 chs.

Note: Loop a short piece of yarn around any stitch to mark Row 1 as **right** side.

Row 2: Ch 1, turn; sc in each hdc and in each ch across changing to Tan in last sc ***(Fig. 3, page 30)***: 181 sc.

Row 3: Ch 2 **(counts as first hdc, now and throughout)**, turn; hdc in next sc, ch 3, ★ skip next 3 sc, hdc in next 3 sc, ch 3; repeat from ★ across to last 5 sc, skip next 3 sc, hdc in last 2 sc: 91 hdc and 90 chs.

Row 4: Ch 1, turn; sc in each hdc and in each ch across changing to Cream in last sc: 181 sc.

Row 5: Ch 1, turn; sc in first 2 sc, working in **front** of previous 2 rows, tr in skipped st **below** next sc, working in **front** of previous 4 rows, dtr in skipped st **below** next sc, working in **front** of previous 2 rows, skip next st from last tr made, tr in next skipped st, ★ skip next 3 sc from last sc made, sc in next sc, work LSC, sc in next sc, working in **front** of previous 2 rows, tr in skipped st **below** next sc, working in **front** of previous 4 rows, dtr in skipped st **below** next sc, working in **front** of previous 2 rows, skip next st from last tr made, tr in next skipped st; repeat from ★ across to last 5 sc, skip next 3 sc from last sc made, sc in last 2 sc.

Row 6: Ch 3 **(counts as first dc)**, turn; dc in next sc and in each st across changing to Brown in last dc: 181 dc.

Row 7: Ch 2, turn; ★ hdc in next 5 dc, ch 1, skip next dc; repeat from ★ across to last 6 dc, hdc in last 6 dc: 152 hdc and 29 chs.

Row 8: Ch 1, turn; sc in each hdc and in each ch across changing to Tan in last sc: 181 sc.

Row 9: Ch 2, turn; hdc in next 4 sc, ch 3, ★ skip next 3 sc, hdc in next 3 sc, ch 3; repeat from ★ across to last 8 sc, skip next 3 sc, hdc in last 5 sc: 94 hdc and 87 chs.

Row 10: Ch 1, turn; sc in each hdc and in each ch across changing to Cream in last sc.

Row 11: Ch 1, turn; sc in first 3 sc, work LSC, sc in next sc, working in **front** of previous 2 rows, tr in skipped sc **below** next sc, working in **front** of previous 4 rows, dtr in skipped dc **below** next sc, working in **front** of previous 2 rows, skip next sc from last tr made, tr in next skipped sc, ★ skip next 3 sc from last sc made, sc in next sc, work LSC, sc in next sc, working in **front** of previous 2 rows, tr in skipped sc **below** next sc, working in **front** of previous 4 rows, dtr in skipped dc **below** next sc, working in **front** of previous 2 rows, skip next sc from last tr made, tr in next skipped sc; repeat from ★ across to last 8 sc, skip 3 sc from last sc made, sc in next sc, work LSC, sc in last 3 sc.

Row 12: Ch 3 **(counts as first dc)**, turn; dc in next sc and in each st across changing to Brown in last dc: 181 dc.

Row 13: Ch 2, turn; hdc in next 2 dc, ch 1, ★ skip next dc, hdc in next 5 dc, ch 1; repeat from ★ across to last 4 dc, skip next dc, hdc in last 3 dc: 151 hdc and 30 chs.

Rows 14-204: Repeat Rows 2-13, 15 times; then repeat Rows 2-12 once **more**, at end of Row 204, change to Tan in last dc.

Border

Rnd 1: Ch 1, turn; 2 sc in first dc, sc in each dc across to last dc, 3 sc in last dc; work 221 sc evenly spaced across ends of rows; working in free loops of beginning ch ***(Fig. 1, page 30)***, 3 sc in first ch, sc in each ch across to marked ch, 3 sc in marked ch, remove marker, work 221 sc evenly spaced across ends of rows, sc in same st as first sc; join with slip st to first sc: 812 sc.

Rnd 2: Ch 2, do **not** turn; hdc in same st as joining and in each sc across to center sc of next corner 3-sc group, 3 hdc in center sc, ★ hdc in each sc across to center sc of next corner 3-sc group, 3 hdc in center sc; repeat from ★ once **more**, hdc in each sc across and in same st as first hdc; join with slip st to first hdc: 820 hdc.

Rnd 3: Ch 3 **(counts as first hdc plus ch 1)**, hdc in same st as joining, ch 1, ★ skip next hdc, (hdc in next hdc, ch 1, skip next hdc) across to center hdc of next corner 3-hdc group, (hdc, ch 1) 3 times in center hdc; repeat from ★ 2 times **more**, skip next hdc, (hdc in next hdc, ch 1, skip next hdc) across, hdc in same st as first hdc, ch 1; join with slip st to first hdc, finish off: 418 hdc and 418 chs.

Rnd 4: With **right** side facing, join Brown with sc in third hdc of any corner 3-hdc group ***(see Joining With Sc, page 30)***; working in **front** of next ch, dc in skipped hdc one rnd **below**, ★ † sc in next hdc, working in **front** of next ch, dc in skipped hdc one rnd **below** †; repeat from † to † across to next corner 3-hdc group, (sc in next hdc, working in **front** of next ch, dc in center hdc one rnd **below**) twice; repeat from ★ around; join with slip st to first sc: 836 sts.

Rnd 5: Ch 2, hdc in next st and in each st around working 5 hdc in center sc of each corner 5-st group; join with slip to first hdc, finish off: 852 hdc.

Rnd 6: With **right** side facing, join Cream with sc in last hdc of any corner 5-hdc group; ★ † work LSC, (sc in next hdc, work LSC) across to next corner 5-hdc group, (sc in next hdc, work LSC in corner sc one rnd **below**) twice †, sc in next hdc; repeat from ★ 2 times **more**; then repeat from † to † once; join with slip st to first sc: 852 sts.

Rnd 7: Ch 1, sc in same st as joining and in each st around; join with slip st to first sc, finish off.

ARROWS

●●○○ EASY

Finished Size: 50" x 76" (127 cm x 193 cm)

Shopping List

Yarn (Medium Weight) MEDIUM 4

(3.5 ounces, 170 yards (100 grams, 156 meters) per skein**)**:

- ☐ Red - 9 skeins
- ☐ Cream - 7 skeins

Crochet Hook

- ☐ Size G (4 mm) **or** size needed for gauge

Gauge Information

In pattern,

2 repeats (20 sts) = 6½" (16.5 cm);

8 rows = 5" (12.75 cm)

Gauge Swatch: 6½" wide x 5" high (16.5 cm x 12.75 cm)

With Cream, ch 21.

Rows 1-8: Work same as Body, page 28: 20 sts.

Finish off.

Stitch Guide

TREBLE CROCHET ***(abbreviated tr)***

YO twice, insert hook in st indicated, YO and pull up a loop (4 loops on hook), (YO and draw through 2 loops on hook) 3 times.

DOUBLE TREBLE CROCHET ***(abbreviated dtr)***

YO 3 times, insert hook in st indicated, YO and pull up a loop (5 loops on hook), (YO and draw through 2 loops on hook) 4 times.

Each row is worked across the length of the Afghan.

Body

With Cream, ch 231.

Row 1 (Right side)**:** Sc in second ch from hook and in next ch, hdc in next 2 chs, dc in next 2 chs, tr in next 2 chs, ★ dtr in next ch, **(**ch 5, slip st in next st **(counts as one dtr, now and throughout))**, sc in next 2 chs, hdc in next 2 chs, dc in next 2 chs, tr in next 2 chs; repeat from ★ across to last 2 chs, dtr in last 2 chs changing to Red in last dtr made ***(Fig. 3, page 30)***: 230 sts.

Note: Loop a short piece of yarn around any stitch to mark Row 1 as **right** side.

Row 2: Ch 1, turn; sc in first 2 dtr, hdc in next 2 tr, dc in next 2 dc, tr in next 2 hdc, dtr in next 2 sc, ★ sc in next 2 dtr, hdc in next 2 tr, dc in next 2 dc, tr in next 2 hdc, dtr in next 2 sc; repeat from ★ across.

Row 3: Ch 5 **(counts as first dtr, now and throughout)**, turn; dtr in next dtr, tr in next 2 tr, dc in next 2 dc, hdc in next 2 hdc, sc in next 2 sc, ★ **(**slip st in next dtr, ch 5 **(counts as one dtr))**, dtr in next dtr, tr in next 2 tr, dc in next 2 dc, hdc in next 2 hdc, sc in next 2 sc; repeat from ★ across changing to Cream in last sc made.

Row 4: Ch 5, turn; dtr in next sc, tr in next 2 hdc, dc in next 2 dc, hdc in next 2 tr, sc in next 2 dtr, ★ dtr in next 2 sc, tr in next 2 hdc, dc in next 2 dc, hdc in next 2 tr, sc in next 2 dtr; repeat from ★ across.

Row 5: Ch 5, turn; dtr in next sc, tr in next 2 hdc, dc in next 2 dc, hdc in next 2 tr, sc in next 2 dtr, ★ slip st in next sc, ch 5, dtr in next sc, tr in next 2 hdc, dc in next 2 dc, hdc in next 2 tr, sc in next 2 dtr; repeat from ★ across changing to Red in last sc made.

Row 6: Ch 5, turn; dtr in next sc, tr in next 2 hdc, dc in next 2 dc, hdc in next 2 tr, sc in next 2 dtr, ★ dtr in next 2 sc, tr in next 2 hdc, dc in next 2 dc, hdc in next 2 tr, sc in next 2 dtr; repeat from ★ across.

Row 7: Ch 1, turn; sc in first 2 sc, hdc in next 2 hdc, dc in next 2 dc, tr in next 2 tr, ★ dtr in next dtr, ch 5, slip st in next dtr, sc in next 2 sc, hdc in next 2 hdc, dc in next 2 dc, tr in next 2 tr; repeat from ★ across to last 2 dtr, dtr in last 2 dtr changing to Cream in last dtr made.

Row 8: Ch 1, turn; sc in first 2 dtr, hdc in next 2 tr, dc in next 2 dc, tr in next 2 hdc, dtr in next 2 sc, ★ sc in next 2 dtr, hdc in next 2 tr, dc in next 2 dc, tr in next 2 hdc, dtr in next 2 sc; repeat from ★ across.

Row 9: Ch 1, turn; sc in first 2 dtr, hdc in next 2 tr, dc in next 2 dc, tr in next 2 hdc, ★ dtr in next sc, ch 5, slip st in next sc, sc in next 2 dtr, hdc in next 2 tr, dc in next 2 dc, tr in next 2 hdc; repeat from ★ across to last 2 sc, dtr in last 2 sc changing to Red in last dtr made.

Rows 10-80: Repeat Rows 2-9, 8 times; then repeat Rows 2-8 once **more**; at end of Row 80, finish off.

Edging

Rnd 1: With **right** side facing, join Red with sc in first dtr on Row 80 ***(see Joining With Sc, page 30)***; 2 sc in same st, sc in each st across to last sc, 3 sc in last sc; working in ends of rows, sc evenly across to beginning ch; working in free loops of beginning ch ***(Fig. 1, page 30)***, 3 sc in first ch, sc in each ch across to ch at base of first sc, 3 sc in ch at base of first sc; working in ends of rows, sc evenly across; join with slip st to first sc.

Rnd 2: Ch 3 **(counts as first dc)**, 5 dc in next sc, dc in next sc and in each sc around working 5 dc in center sc of each corner 3-sc group; join with slip st to first dc, finish off.

GENERAL INSTRUCTIONS

Abbreviations

BPdc	Back Post double crochet(s)
ch(s)	chain(s)
cm	centimeters
dc	double crochet(s)
dtr	double treble crochet(s)
ex LSC	extra Long Single Crochet(s)
FPdc	Front Post double crochet(s)
hdc	half double crochet(s)
LSC	Long Single Crochet(s)
mm	millimeters
Rnd(s)	Round(s)
sc	single crochet(s)
sc2tog	single crochet 2 together
sp(s)	space(s)
st(s)	stitch(es)
tr	treble crochet(s)
YO	yarn over

Symbols & Terms

★ — work instructions following ★ as many **more** times as indicated in addition to the first time.

† to † — work all instructions from first † to second † **as many** times as specified.

( ) or **[ ]**— work enclosed instructions **as many** times as specified by the number immediately following **or** work all enclosed instructions in the stitch or space indicated **or** contains explanatory remarks.

colon (:) — the number(s) given after a colon at the end of a row or round denote(s) the number of stitches or spaces you should have on that row or round.

Gauge

Exact gauge is **essential** for proper size. Before beginning your Afghan, make the sample swatch given in the individual instructions in the yarn and hook specified. After completing the swatch, measure it, counting your stitches and rows or rounds carefully. If your swatch is larger or smaller than specified, **make another, changing hook size to get the correct gauge**. Keep trying until you find the size hook that will give you the specified gauge.

●○○○ **BEGINNER**	Projects for first-time crocheters using basic stitches. Minimal shaping.
●●○○ **EASY**	Projects using yarn with basic stitches, repetitive stitch patterns, simple color changes, and simple shaping and finishing.
●●●○ **INTERMEDIATE**	Projects using a variety of techniques, such as basic lace patterns or color patterns, mid-level shaping and finishing.
●●●● **EXPERIENCED**	Projects with intricate stitch patterns, techniques and dimension, such as non-repeating patterns, multi-color techniques, fine threads, small hooks, detailed shaping and refined finishing.

CROCHET TERMINOLOGY		
UNITED STATES		INTERNATIONAL
slip stitch (slip st)	=	single crochet (sc)
single crochet (sc)	=	double crochet (dc)
half double crochet (hdc)	=	half treble crochet (htr)
double crochet (dc)	=	treble crochet (tr)
treble crochet (tr)	=	double treble crochet (dtr)
double treble crochet (dtr)	=	triple treble crochet (ttr)
triple treble crochet (tr tr)	=	quadruple treble crochet (qtr)
skip	=	miss

CROCHET HOOKS																
U.S.	B-1	C-2	D-3	E-4	F-5	G-6	7	H-8	I-9	J-10	K-10½	L-11	M/N-13	N/P-15	P/Q	Q	S
Metric - mm	2.25	2.75	3.25	3.5	3.75	4	4.5	5	5.5	6	6.5	8	9	10	15	16	19

Joining With Sc

When instructed to join with sc, begin with a slip knot on hook. Insert hook in stitch or space indicated, YO and pull up a loop, YO and draw through both loops on hook.

Free Loops of a Chain

When instructed to work in free loops of a chain, work in loop indicated by arrow ***(Fig. 1)***.

Fig. 1

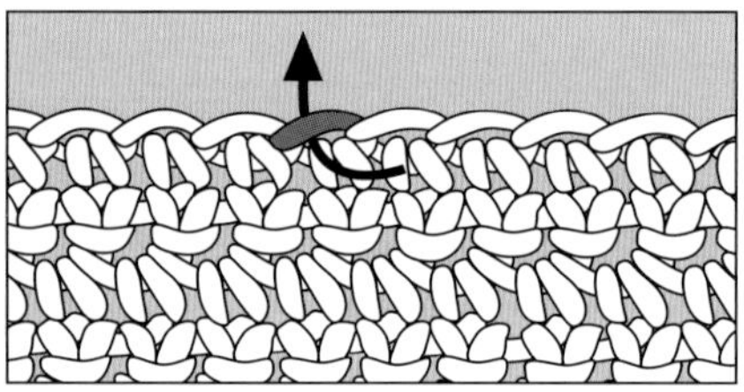

Back Loop Only

Work only in loop(s) indicated by arrow ***(Fig. 2)***.

Fig. 2

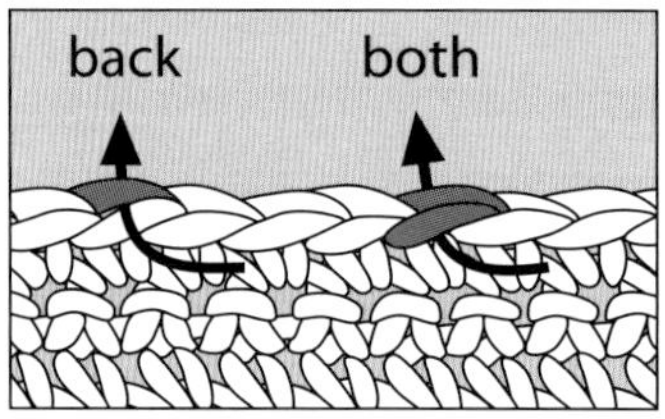

Changing Color

Work last stitch to within one step of completion, hook new yarn ***(Fig. 3)*** and draw through both loops on hook. Cut old yarn and work over both ends.

Fig. 3

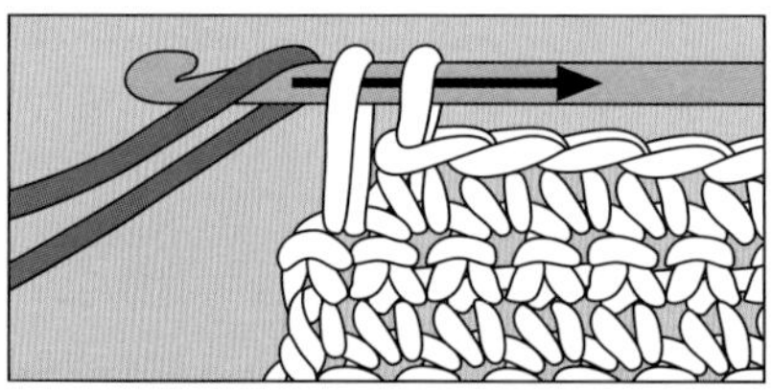

Reverse Single Crochet

(abbreviated reverse sc)

Working from **left** to **right**, ★ insert hook in st to right of hook ***(Fig. 4a)***, YO and draw through, under and to left of loop on hook (2 loops on hook) ***(Fig. 4b)***, YO and draw through both loops on hook ***(Fig. 4c)*** **(reverse sc made, *Fig. 4d*)**; repeat from ★ around.

Fig. 4a

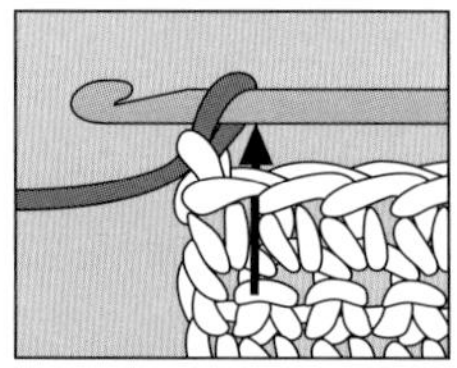

Fig. 4b

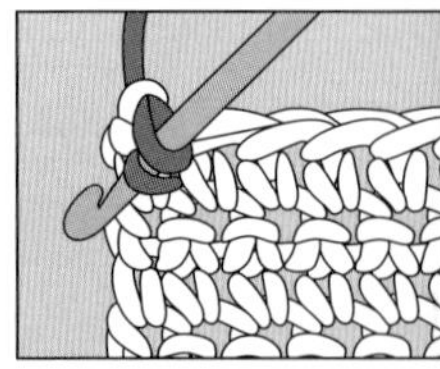

Fig. 4c

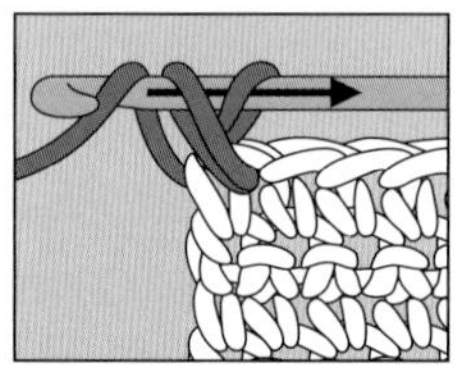

Fig. 4d

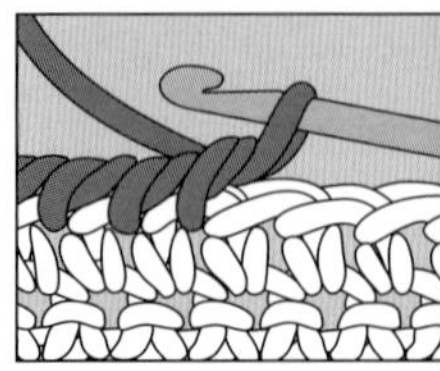

Yarn Weight Symbol & Names	LACE 0	SUPER FINE 1	FINE 2	LIGHT 3	MEDIUM 4	BULKY 5	SUPER BULKY 6	JUMBO 7
Type of Yarns in Category	Fingering, size 10 crochet thread	Sock, Fingering, Baby	Sport, Baby	DK, Light Worsted	Worsted, Afghan, Aran	Chunky, Craft, Rug	Super Bulky, Roving	Jumbo, Roving
Crochet Gauge* Ranges in Single Crochet to 4" (10 cm)	32-42 sts**	21-32 sts	16-20 sts	12-17 sts	11-14 sts	8-11 sts	6-9 sts	5 sts and fewer
Advised Hook Size Range	Steel*** 6 to 8, Regular hook B-1	B-1 to E-4	E-4 to 7	7 to I-9	I-9 to K-10½	K-10½ to M/N-13	M/N-13 to Q	Q and larger

*GUIDELINES ONLY: The chart above reflects the most commonly used gauges and hook sizes for specific yarn categories.

** Lace weight yarns are usually crocheted with larger hooks to create lacy openwork patterns. Accordingly, a gauge range is difficult to determine. Always follow the gauge stated in your pattern.

*** Steel crochet hooks are sized differently from regular hooks–the higher the number, the smaller the hook, which is the reverse of regular hook sizing.

YARN INFORMATION

Each afghan in this book was made using Medium Weight Yarn. Any brand of Medium Weight Yarn may be used. It is best to refer to the yardage/meters when determining how many balls or skeins to purchase. Remember, to arrive at the finished size, it is the GAUGE/TENSION that is important, not the brand of yarn.

For your convenience, listed below are the specific yarns used to create our photography models. Because yarn manufacturers make frequent changes in their product lines, you may sometimes find it necessary to use a substitute yarn or to search for the discontinued product at alternate suppliers (locally or online).

ZIPPERS

Red Heart® Super Saver®

Green - #624 Tea Leaf

Dk Green - #406 Medium Thyme

LIGHTNING BOLTS

Premier® Yarns Deborah Norville Collection™ Everyday®

Cream - #02 Cream

Green - #31 Peacock

SKYLINE

Patons® Décor™

Grey - #87671 Pale Grey Heather

Navy - #87643 Navy

OCEAN WAVES

Caron® Simply Soft®

White - #9701 White

Lt Blue - #9709 Light Country Blue

Dk Blue - #9711 Dark Country Blue

Blue - #9710 Country Blue

RIPPLES

Red Heart® Soft®

Dk Grey - #9010 Charcoal

Black - #4614 Black

Lt Grey - #9440 Light Grey Heather

SHADED VEES

Lion Brand® Heartland®

Cream - #098 Acadia

Tan - #122 Grand Canyon

Brown - #125 Mammoth Cave

ARROWS

Lion Brand® Vanna's Choice®

Red - #180 Cranberry

Cream - #098 Fisherman

We have made every effort to ensure that these instructions are accurate and complete. We cannot, however, be responsible for human error, typographical mistakes, or variations in individual work.

Afghans made and instructions tested by Janet Akins, Raymelle Greening, Amanda Loggins, and Barbara Schou.

Production Team: Instructional/Technical Editor - Sarah J. Green; Editorial Writer - Susan Frantz Wiles; Senior Graphic Artist - Lora Puls; Graphic Artist - Kytanna McFarlin; Photo Stylist - Lori Wenger; and Photographers - Lily Darragh and Ken West.

MEET
JANET L. AKINS

Janet L. Akins is a longtime crochet pattern tester for Leisure Arts. She learned to crochet at the age of 13. "I remember my Grandma teaching me this skill one summer on her front porch," she says. "I've enjoyed crocheting leisurely and professionally in my later years."

She especially enjoys making afghans but occasionally has branched out into crocheting shawls, dolls, rugs, hats, and other projects.

"I tend to gravitate toward beginner patterns mostly because I enjoy creating something that many others can make," she says. "I definitely like to test patterns out to see if they are cute yet can be completed easily."

Her special interest in geometric patterns was her inspiration for the graphic afghans in this book. "The patterns are applicable for all ages. They can be used in a nursery, kids' room, college room, or family room to match any decor."

Janet has two grown children and two grandsons. She enjoys biking, playing tennis, bowling, and doing DIY home projects with her children.